Images of Superior & Douglas County

*P*hotographs provided by the Douglas County Historical Society.

COVER PICTURE:
Roth Brother's Department Store fire, May 24, 1911.

AT LEFT:
The Keystone National Bank Building, 714 Tower Avenue, c. 1915.

BACK COVER:
Fairlawn Mansion, c. 1895

PUBLISHED BY:
**The Douglas County Historical Society
Preservation Committee**
James Brew - Chairperson, Joseph Moline, Charles Cieslak

Staff
Rachael Martin, Executive Director
Joseph Korman, Collections Manager
♦
PRINTED BY:
Arrowhead Printing, Inc.

ISBN 0-9664281-1-0
January 1998
Douglas County Historical Society

Arrival of the First Street Cars in South Superior, September 14, 1892.

The Davidson Windmill, Hwy. 13, c.1910.

Stage Departing for St. Paul, 1870.

President William McKinley speaking at the West Superior City Hall, October, 1899.

The Normandy Block, 1425-1429 Tower Avenue, c. 1928.

The Massachusetts Block, 1525-1531 Tower Avenue, c. 1910.

700 Block of Tower Avenue looking North, c. 1880.

300 Block of Tower Avenue looking South, 1889.

The West Superior Hotel, Corner of Tower Avenue and Belknap Street, c.1891.

The Empire Block, 1202-1204 Tower Avenue, c.1895.

1200 Block of Towwr Avenue looking North, c.1910.

The Maryland (right) and Wemyss (left) Blocks, 1223-1227 and 1301-1305 Tower Avenue, c.1910.

The National Bank of Commerce Building, 1123 Tower Avenue, c.1915.

The Grand Opera House, 1713-1715 Belknap Street, 1889.

Douglas County Court House (left) and Jail (right) 5th Street and Newton Ave., c.1895.

Conner's Point Fire Hall, c.1890.

Superior Police Department, Hammond Avenue and Broadway, c.1913.

Miss Mary McMahon's School House, 1895.

St. Mary's Hospital, 1017 Clough Avenue, c.1900.

Hawthorne Depot, c.1890.

James G. Blaine High School, Hughitt Avenue and 14th Street, c.1900.

St. Stanislaus Catholic Church, 14th Street and Birch Avenue, 1916.

Nelson Dewey High School, Thompson Avenue and 6th Street, c. 1890.

West Superior Union Depot, Oakes Avenue and Broadway, c.1890.

Concordia Lutheran Church, John Avenue and 17th Street, c.1891.

State Normal School, Grand Avenue between 17th and 18th Streets, c.1900

West Superior Union Depot, Oakes Avenue and Broadway, c.1910.

Superior Central High School, 1015 Belknap Street, 1910.

The Peyton-Kimball-Barber Sawmill, Conner's Point, c.1880.

The Russell-Miller Milling Company, c.1910.

The Listman (left), Anchor (center), and Daisy (right) Mills, c.1913.

Hans Johnson's Lumber Camp, Douglas County, c.1888.

A. W. Kunert's Tin Shop, 273 West 2nd Street, c.1870.

Lumber Camp, Douglas County, c.1880.

Duluth-Superior Street Railway Car Barn, 4th Street and Ogden Avenue, c.1890.

4th of July Parade, Broadway and Tower Avenue, 1896.

Launching of the S.S. Pontiers, Superior Shipbuilding Company, November 1916.

The American Steel Barge Company, November 1891.

41

The Russell Block, 1608 Tower Avenue, c.1910.

The Berkshire Block, 917-927 Tower Avenue, c.1910.

The New Jersey Block, Tower Avenue and Belknap Street, c.1928.

Board of Trade Building, 1507 Tower Avenue, c.1895.

James Ritche's Farm, Superior City, June 20, 1870.

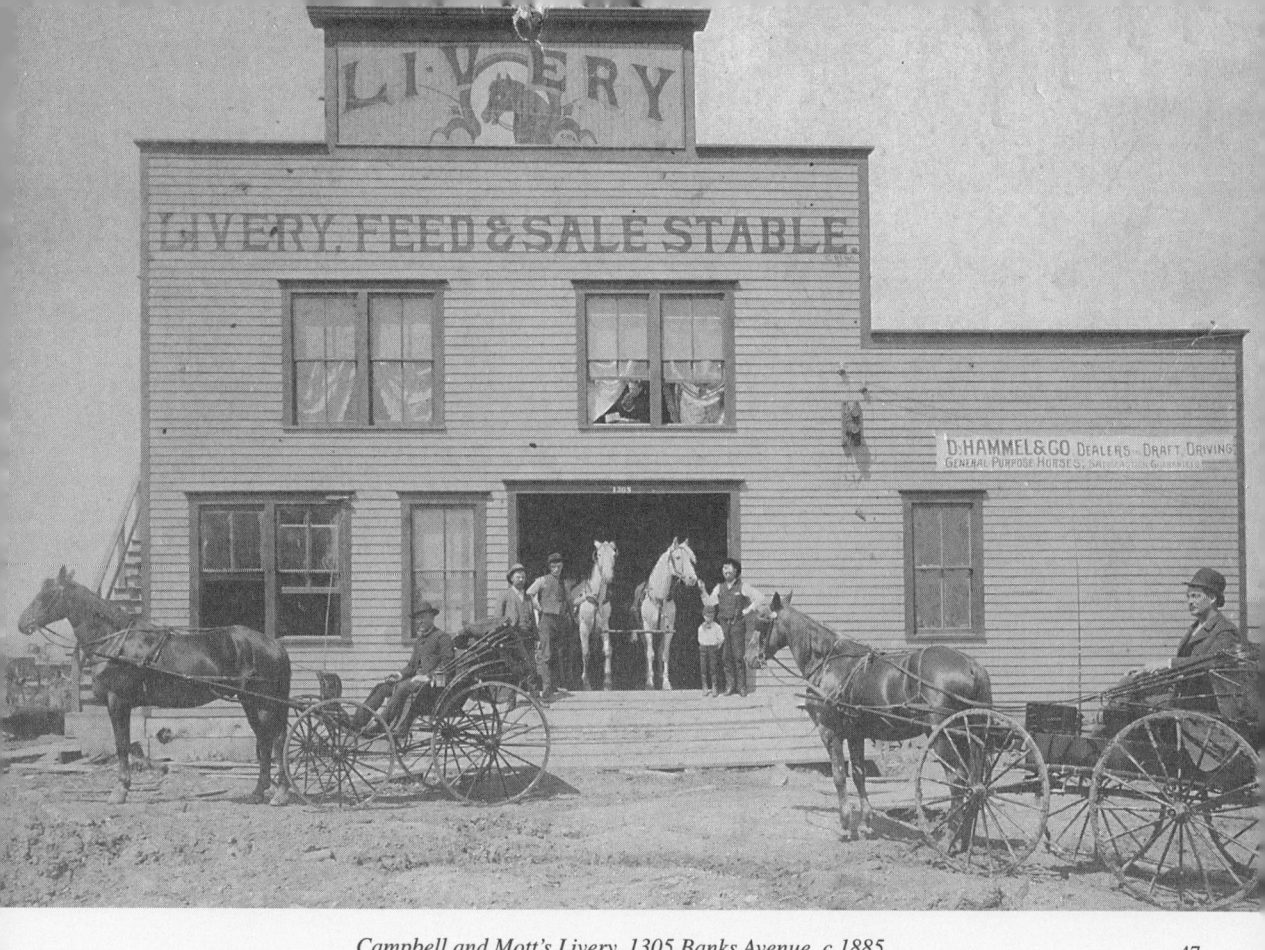

Campbell and Mott's Livery, 1305 Banks Avenue, c.1885.

Laying Track near Allouez Bay, c.1885.

Lackawanna Avenue and 19th Street, looking west, 1902.

St. James Hotel, Tower and Central Avenues, 1892.

S.S. Christopher Columbus, 1893.

Lake Nebagamain Ice Company, c.1890.

Bill Gordon's Hotel, Gordon, WI, 1887.

The Superior Shipbuilding Company Dry Dock, c.1900.

The First Threshing Machine in Douglas County, 1885.

56   *The Steamer North Star loading flour at the Eastern Minnesota Flour Sheds, West Superior, c.1880.*

Lehigh Coal Docks, West Superior, c.1885.

C.S.P.M. & O. locomotive #211 at the Great Northern Elevators, c.1880.

Daniel Friedman & Joseph Argeneau's Grocery, Cass Avenue and 2nd Street, c.1889.

Silver Dave's Sample Room, 58th Street and Tower Avenue, c.1910.

Eimon's Mechantile Company, 413 Banks Avenue, c.1895.

The Frey Block, 519 Tower Avenue, c.1887.